Contents

Introducing Clachtoll Broch Project

Over two thousand years ago, Clachtoll Broch stood proud on Scotland's north-west coast. The imposing drystone building, circular in plan, was the family home at the heart of a productive and self-sustaining farmstead in the Iron Age. It was destroyed by a catastrophic fire at the beginning of the first century AD. Walls tumbled down and rubble lay where it fell, undisturbed for almost two millennia.

By the early years of this century, the ruinous remains of the broch were moving ever closer to collapse. Winter storms crashed over the walls, picking apart the broch's structure and pulling it, stone by stone, into the sea. Further stonework was dislodged by intrepid explorers clambering over the ruins. As the years passed, Clachtoll Broch's future looked precarious, and the monument grew ever more dangerous for visitors. Local community group Historic Assynt stepped in to change that.

Historic Assynt is a community-led organisation that was set up in 1998 with the goal of conserving the ruins of Ardvreck Castle and Calda House, and restoring the former Parish Kirk in the medieval heart of Assynt at Inchnadamph.

As local concern about the state of the broch grew, Historic Assynt agreed to co-host a public meeting with other concerned groups.

Clachtoll Broch

Lochinver
Ullapool

One of Historic Assynt's founding goals was to conserve Ardvreck Castle (foreground) and Calda House

*Historic Assynt undertook survey across the parish
as part of Assynt's Hidden Lives Project, 2009-2010*

Survey at Loch Borralan East chambered cairn, 2009

Dun Carloway, on the Isle of Lewis

That meeting revealed widespread worry about the safety of the broch and its visitors, but also a desire to find out more about the broch's origins and use, to improve public access, and to provide visitors with more information about the site. Historic Assynt left the meeting tasked with seeking funding for a feasibility study. And so began a close relationship between Historic Assynt and Clachtoll Broch, which is ongoing nearly 16 years later!

The feasibility study suggested that the broch was even more unstable than first thought. Historic Scotland (now Historic Environment Scotland) commissioned and funded a Conservation Management Plan by AOC Archaeology Group. AOC's work highlighted that more intervention was required, some urgently, and some to ensure the building's longer-term survival. However, much of the work required would expose underlying archaeological material. Historic Assynt had to come up with a plan that would combine repair, consolidation and excavation, while at the same time enhancing access to reduce visitors' temptation to clamber over the ruins, and so prevent further damage to the broch.

The broch full to the brim with rubble on the first day of the excavations

The first phase of work at Clachtoll was delivered as part of 'Life and Death in Assynt's Past', which focussed on excavation and consolidation work at three very different sites: a Neolithic cairn by Loch Borralan; Clachtoll's Iron Age broch; and an 18th century longhouse in the cleared township of Glenleraig. The work at Clachtoll stabilised the dangerous entrance passage and provided valuable insights into the structure's condition, as well as providing some intriguing pointers to part of its complex story.

Clachtoll Broch's future looked precarious until Historic Assynt stepped in

For the first time, Historic Assynt got a glimpse of the broch's dramatic demise. John Barber and his colleagues from AOC identified evidence of a significant collapse, possibly associated with a fire. Charcoal found on an internal ledge provided a date between the mid first century BC and the mid first century AD, firmly within the Iron Age. It became clear that Clachtoll was unique: traces of the lives of the last inhabitants were, in all likelihood, lying undisturbed beneath by the rubble that filled the interior of the broch. The project presented an extraordinary opportunity to explore Iron Age life.

Following the conservation work, engineering students at the University of Edinburgh, under the direction of Dr Dimitris Theodossopoulos, carried out modelling of the surviving remains. Their tests, using scale models of the broch, indicated that the rubble in the interior was exerting constant pressure on the surviving walls, pushing them outwards. The threat of total collapse seemed more and more likely, and the need to excavate and consolidate the broch became essential.

The outcome of all of this preparatory work was an ambitious plan of action. In 2017, Historic Assynt's years of preparation came to fruition with a formidable project to fully excavate the interior of the broch, while carrying out repairs to the stonework. This monumental feat was carried out as part of Coigach & Assynt Living Landscape, a landscape partnership project which aimed to bring environmental and economic benefits to the Coigach and Assynt regions of north-west Scotland.

Historic Assynt maintained steady communication with the local community throughout, and their ideas and wishes were fed into the design of the final project.

Historic Assynt is immensely grateful for the help, support and involvement of a huge number of organisations and individuals over the years, listed below. Many, many thanks to one and all!

Gordon Sleight
Historic Assynt Project Leader

Icons of the Iron Age

Brochs are drystone towers, built in Scotland in the Iron Age. The first brochs were built at least as early as the 4th century BC. The buildings were often remodelled and reused over the centuries, and at some sites, villages grew up around the low remains of the towers in the later Iron Age period. There are more than 600 known and possible brochs, particularly densely clustered in the Northern Isles, Western Isles, and northern mainland Scotland.

Brochs have several distinguishing features, yet no two brochs are identical. They are circular in plan and were usually designed to be tower-like in their proportions. They feature a unique twin-walled method of construction. Within the thickness of the walls at ground level are small rooms, known as cells, and a set of stairs which spiral upwards. Brochs have one low doorway, sometimes topped with a large triangular lintel stone, and no windows.

Inside, a central hearth provided light and heat and a focal point for activity. A ledge around the inner circumference, known as a scarcement ledge, provided support for upper storeys or platforms, perhaps floored with woven wattle panels. How brochs were roofed is a subject of much debate since no broch roofs survive, but they were most likely thatched, perhaps with reeds, bracken, heather or straw, and perhaps with a turf component,

depending on what was available locally. The tallest standing broch is at Mousa on Shetland, which survives to around 13m high. Most are much more ruinous, reduced to their lowest few metres. Aside from Mousa, the best-preserved examples are the others of the 'big five': Dun Carloway on Lewis, Dun Dornadilla in northern Sutherland, and the Glenelg brochs of Dun Telve and Dun Troddan.

Iron Age buildings were all about the wow factor: social status was conveyed through architecture

Building a broch required significant resources, both in terms of materials and labour. Brochs were traditionally interpreted as the homes of Iron Age tribal chieftains since these powerful leaders could have wielded enough power to command the build. However, Iron Age society in the north of Britain may have been made up of relatively egalitarian groups, unlike the very hierarchical society of the medieval period. Brochs are now more widely understood to have been the homes of farming families, probably multi-generational extended families. It is possible that bonds between communities, perhaps alliances formed through marriage, might have seen families work together: "we'll help you build your broch this year if you help us with ours next year".

Despite their towering appearance, which might invite comparison with castles, brochs are not well designed to withstand attack, and it is improbable that this was their primary function. They were designed to look impressive. Iron Age buildings were all about the wow factor: from hillforts to brochs and crannogs, social status was conveyed through architecture.

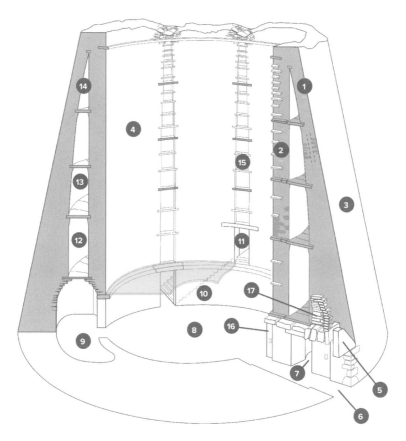

Brochs display a range of key structural components

1 Outer Wall	10 Stair
2 Inner Wall	11 First floor entrance
3 Outer wall face	12 First floor galleries
4 Inner wall face	13 Second floor galleries
5 Large lintel over entrance	14 Inter-mural galleries
6 Entrance passage	15 Stacked void
7 Guard cell	16 Inner lining wall
8 Circular interior	17 Cell over entrance passage
9 Corbelled cell	

Construction of a broch was a complex task. Their tower-like proportions are challenging to achieve using nothing but un-mortared, dry stone. Broch-building probably required the involvement of an experienced master mason or architect, perhaps a travelling expert who oversaw a team of local labourers. Often, brochs display evidence of remodelling and repair, showing that they were prone to structural failures such as cracking lintels as the colossal weight of their walls settled.

These distinctive Iron Age buildings are unique to Scotland

Other huge, circular structures are broch-like in appearance but don't meet the modern criteria that archaeologists use to decide whether a building can be considered a broch or not. These monumental roundhouses often display characteristics that link them to local building styles, demonstrating how people played around with the "rules" of broch-building to create something that reflected their values. Doon Castle Broch in Dumfries and Galloway, for example, has two entrances, which is at odds with the traditional broch model, but in keeping with the roundhouse tradition in the area. Other brochs in the south of Scotland are similarly unusual: Edin's Hall in the Scottish Borders is laid out with the plan of a broch, but has such a large diameter that the finished building was probably never tower-like. These outlier brochs probably show that the symbol of the broch was one of strength and power in Iron Age society, and was emulated by groups outside the main broch-building zones.

These distinctive Iron Age buildings are unique to Scotland. Each was home to a family or community with its own story. What follows is Clachtoll's story.

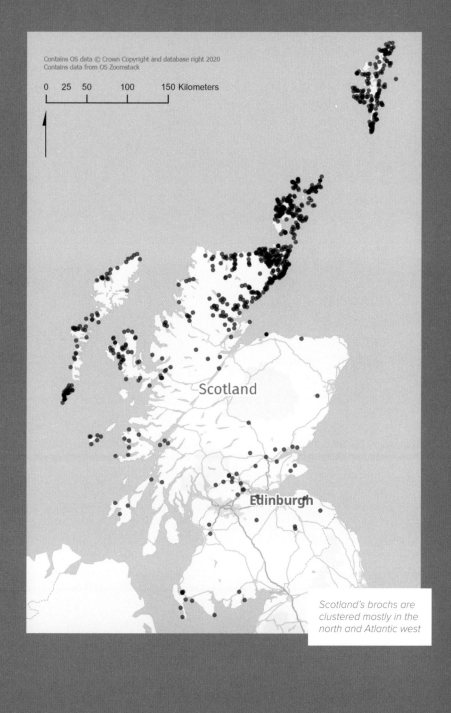

0   25   50   100   150 Kilometers

Scotland

Edinburgh

Scotland's brochs are clustered mostly in the north and Atlantic west

Clachtoll Broch: Setting, Structure and Collapse

The Wider Landscape

Clachtoll Broch was first depicted on a map in the 1770s, marked as 'Old Castle' on Home's Survey of Assynt. It is noted in the Ordnance Survey Name Books in the 1870s as An Dùn, Gaelic for "the fort".

Sitting high on an exposed rocky knoll at the southern end of Stoer Bay, the broch now stands up to 3m tall in some places. The seaward side has been slowly but surely eaten away by the waves with every winter storm, but over three quarters of the broch's ring-shaped footprint survives. Rubble covers the ground on the landward side, a mixture of collapse from the broch tower and also the remains of smaller, ancillary structures and a boundary wall. These have never been excavated, so little is known about the buildings outside the broch.

The landscape around the broch is rough and rocky. Though tree cover is sparse today, they would have been more widespread in the Iron Age: probably mostly birch and hazel, with some pine. People began clearing trees for farming in the Neolithic after 6000 BC, and this would have continued in the Iron Age (800 BC to 400 AD). Good agricultural land is not common in the north-west Highlands, and Iron Age settlements tend to cluster around the better soils, like the machair of Clachtoll and Stoer bays. There are areas to the north of the broch that might have been candidates for the cultivation of barley, which we know from the excavated evidence was grown in abundance. The land to the east and south-east of the broch may have been boggy or even entirely underwater.

John Home's Survey of Assynt in 1774 marks the broch as "Old Castle"

Reddened, burnt deposits in the sequence of successive hearths

A stone lamp in near perfect condition, soon after discovery

The Glowing Heart

The broch's interior was once full of rubble, but the excavations emptied the site to bedrock. Visitors can now walk through the doorway, along the entrance passage, and into the broch itself.

The entrance into the broch is topped by a huge triangular lintel. A low, dark passage leads through the massively thick walls. On either side, you can see the vertical slabs that form the door jambs, and behind them a long hollow slot that would have held a sliding wooden bar, used to secure the door. To either side are small rooms that were traditionally known as guard cells, though there is no evidence to suggest that they were used in this way. At Clachtoll, the cell on the left appears to have been used as a midden or dump towards the end of the broch's use; how the right-hand cell was used is not clear, but it may have been a storage space. There is no evidence, from Clachtoll or elsewhere, that cells were used as living spaces.

The interior of the broch is a circular space around 8.2m in diameter. At the centre is a huge hearth, the heart of the home and a focal point for cooking, craft activities, storytelling and, of course, keeping warm. The hearth was set on a massive stone slab, and was repeatedly remodelled and replaced. The final version was surrounded by a stone kerb forming a working platform, with upright stones at the corners.

Additional light was thrown out by lamps in bowl-shaped vessels made of stone. Scientific analysis of burnt residues on these vessels shows that some of them bear traces of dairy fats, perhaps butter, which may have been used with beeswax as fuel for lighting. Slivers of Scots pine, some with evidence of burning at the tips, might represent fir-candles which remained in use in the Highlands and Islands into the eighteenth century.

These slivers of Scots pine may have been used like candles

Stone bowls like this were used as lamps, with butter and perhaps beeswax as fuel

Treading Carefully

Part of the bedrock of the knoll was quarried to even it out a little before the broch was built. However, it remains uneven, stepping down from west to east. This rough floor surface was covered with a carpet of sorts: reeds, rushes and grasses were laid down, and mixed with these was sand, ash and gravel. Close analysis of the floor deposits showed that conditions underfoot were often wet and probably quite unpleasant. Throwing down vegetation and sand or ash probably improved the situation a little. This accumulation of material also provided the perfect environment for the survival of lost things, little objects that were dropped and forgotten, only to be found by archaeologists many centuries later. The flooring was occasionally renewed – we might imagine a thorough spring clean – and each time, a layer of evidence relating to life at the broch was thrown out as rubbish. As a result, the information provided by the floor deposits at Clachtoll really does represent a snapshot of life in the broch at the very end of its life cycle.

A steep drop in the bedrock at the south-east side of the interior was exploited to create an under-floor storage compartment. We might compare this feature to the souterrains (sometimes called 'earth houses'), Iron Age underground chambers or passages found across Scotland. They are thought to have been used for food storage, a bit like cellars.

A steep drop in the bedrock at the south-east side of the interior was exploited to create an under-floor storage compartment

Kubiena tins are used to collect soil samples, retaining the stratigraphic sequence of the layered deposits

The souterrain, or underground storage area, with quern stone in the floor

The broch is accessed via a low doorway, topped by a huge triangular lintel

Within the Walls

A doorway on the southern side of the interior gives access to a staircase. Stone steps curve upwards in a clockwise direction within the thickness of the wall, ending in a landing that would once have led into an upper storey, perhaps a mezzanine-like arrangement made from woven wattle screens.

Other doorways give access to cells within the walls, seemingly used for storage of grain. One of these was accessed a little above ground level; a ladder or steps may have been used to get in and out of the space. These small spaces have dual purposes: they provide space for storage or rubbish disposal, while also

reducing the weight of the tower-like wall. Stacked voids, vertical gaps in the stonework which look like pigeon-holes, are visible in the upper interior of many brochs that stand taller than Clachtoll, and they serve a similar purpose: to relieve pressure on the vulnerable lintels over doorways.

The stairs within the thick broch wall would once have given access to an upper storey

Exceptional preservation within the broch allowed for the discovery of carbonised plant remains like these

Fire!

The broch's interior deposits were covered by a thick layer of burnt material, the result of a massive fire that probably occurred in the early years of the first century AD. The roof and internal fittings fell inwards as they burned, sealing in artefacts and floor deposits under a protective layer of ash and carbonised wood. It looks as though the fire took the broch's occupants by surprise: sickles and scythes were left leaning against the wall; sheaves of barley were left to char in their storerooms within the walls.

There's no evidence that anyone was killed in the fire, nor is there any sign of an attempt to repair or salvage the building. The broch was abandoned and its occupants never returned, the last traces of their lives left beneath the rubble and ash for archaeologists to excavate some two thousand years later. It is impossible to know whether this fire was an accident or the result of an attack, perhaps by a neighbouring group or by raiders, but the fact that no one attempted to recover the settlement suggests that the occupants of Clachtoll were forced to move on.

One of the intra-mural cells: small rooms within the thickness of the broch walls

An Ever-changing Entity

The broch as we see it today is only one version of Clachtoll Broch, the broch's final form.

Clues within the stonework tell us that the building had been remodelled on numerous occasions. The triangular lintel above the door, for example, does not seem to be in its original position but rather is turned onto its side, marking an area of repair to the outer wall face. Inside the broch, at the south-east, bulging stonework near the base of the wall forms a rough ledge. Above this level, the stonework is markedly neater and built on a different alignment. It is likely that the chaotic lower stonework represents the footing of an earlier building - probably a broch with a very similar layout – that collapsed in the Early Iron Age. The neater stonework above represents the rebuild.

The huge amounts of rubble around the broch (and, prior to excavation, within the broch) show that the broch was once much taller. However, in its final incarnation, we believe the building at Clachtoll to have been a rather squat structure, not the iconic multi-storeyed tower that the term 'broch' brings to mind.

1 This cell was floored with grasses, reeds and rushes, over which was a layer of flagstones. No finds were discovered in this cell, making it difficult to establish what it was used for.

2 Entrance passage

3 Door jambs

4 This cell appears to have been used as a midden or rubbish dump

5 This cell was used for storing grain

6 Stairs

7 Knocking stone, for removing tough husks from grain

8 The scarcement ledge around the inner circumference of the broch probably once supported an upper storey or platform of some kind

9 Kerb around the hearth, perhaps marking the edge of an activity area

10 Hearth

11 This section is lost, worn away by 2000 years of waves and weather

12 Stone box, perhaps a tank which might have held water if it had a lining

13 Underground storage space

Many brochs were reused in antiquity, repeatedly remodelled and reoccupied over the centuries before eventually falling into disrepair and being left to the elements. Clachtoll's unusual end – the catastrophic fire that forced its occupants out – and the fact that it was never reoccupied makes its excavation entirely unique. The evidence uncovered represents the entirety of a single occupation sequence within the broch, a snapshot of the final fifty years' use of the site, undisturbed for two thousand years.

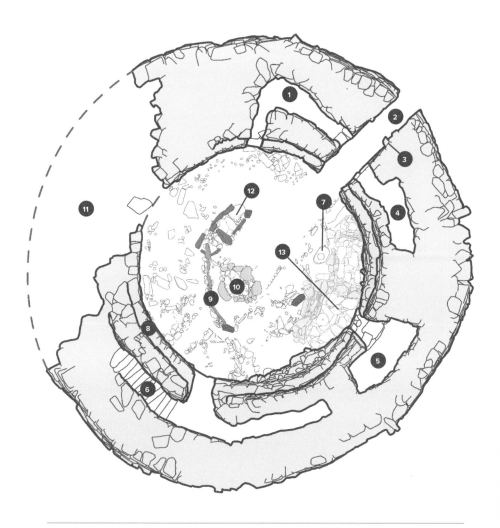

This reconstruction illustration shows Clachtoll Broch as it may have appeared from the outside, with cutaway detail to show the interior. The broch is not depicted as tower-like in its proportions because evidence from the excavations suggests that it was most likely a rather squat building at the end of its life, perhaps a little ragged around the edges.

A substantial wall enclosed the broch; the massive boulders that marked the entrance are still visible in the rubble that surrounds the broch today. There were a few outbuildings, though these have not been excavated so we don't know how they were used – we might imagine them to have functioned as workshops or farm buildings.

The illustration was produced by Chris Mitchell following discussions with AOC's archaeologists. It combines archaeological evidence with artistic license to add interest to our vision of how Clachtoll Broch might have looked in the Iron Age.

Food and Farming

We can explore the economy of Iron Age Clachtoll through the plant and animal remains uncovered during the excavations: cereal remains, nuts, fruits, vegetables and bones all form pieces of the puzzle.

The people of the broch were farmers first and foremost. Almost everything they wanted or needed could be grown, reared, caught or gathered from the land- and seascape surrounding the broch. Meals were cooked around the huge central hearth: it's tempting to picture meat roasting above the flames; fish wrapped in clay and baked in the embers; bubbling stews and soups, and milk warming in clay pots set around the edges of the fire.

The cattle at Clachtoll might have looked a bit like this one, stocky and long-haired

Cereal Crops

The main crop grown by Clachtoll's farmers was hulled barley. Several iron agricultural implements, including sickles, scythes and reaping hooks were found in the broch, lying close together near the broch wall. Perhaps they were stored in a cluster, leaning against the broch wall, and that is where they remained as the broch burned around them.

The people of the broch were farmers first and foremost

Iron reaping hooks, used when gathering crops at harvest

Barley was the primary crop grown at Clachtoll

A rotary quern stone, used for grinding grain into flour

Hulled barley has a tough husk which has to be removed prior to grinding the grain into flour. A 'knocking stone' was found at the broch: a boulder with a cup-shaped hollow in the top that was used like a giant mortar and pestle. Grain was placed in the hollow and bashed to remove the husk. The knocking stone was chock-full of barley when it was found, adding weight to the theory that the broch was abandoned in a hurry. Numerous rotary quern stones were found at the broch, used to grind grain into flour. When they broke, some of the quern stones were reused as building material.

A small fragment of an unfinished wooden bowl, perhaps intended for preparing or serving food

A knocking stone
and numerous
quern stones were
found at the broch

*The knocking stone was full
to the brim with burnt grain*

Meat and Milk

Cattle and sheep were key to the economy at Clachtoll. The animals were kept until they reached their full size. They would have grazed the land nearby and, in the winter, eaten fodder grown on the farm and perhaps seaweed gathered from the shore. They provided milk, a valuable resource for making butter and cheese.

The animals were slaughtered for their meat once they reached optimum size. Most of the sheep were slaughtered between 9 and 16 months, perhaps to reduce the number of excess males in the flock, or as a tactical reduction in flock size in the run-up to winner, to save on fodder. Those that were kept for longer remained with the flock until they were around 30 months old and had reached skeletal maturity. Cattle were kept for longer, most being slaughtered between 18 and 36 months. Though cattle required more fodder than sheep in the lean winter months, they earned their keep by producing more milk, as well as being useful for pulling ploughs and perhaps carts.

Pork was definitely on the menu at Clachtoll, but perhaps only occasionally. Unlike cattle and sheep, pigs don't provide any secondary resources; they can't be milked, nor shorn for their wool. Rearing pigs would have been a costly undertaking, and this may be why pork formed a much smaller part of the diet at Clachtoll than beef and lamb/mutton. Perhaps it was eaten only at feasts or celebrations.

Several animal bones found at the broch were smashed open to extract the marrow. While the people living at Clachtoll seem to have had plenty to eat, they weren't going to waste a tasty and nutritious foodstuff for the sake of a little extra effort.

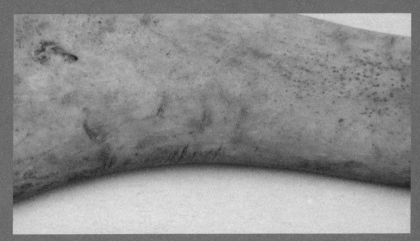

Tiny knife marks on animal bones, left behind by the butcher's knife

Cattle and sheep were key to the economy at Clachtoll

The sheep at Clachtoll were small and hardy, like today's Shetland sheep

Fishing, Foraging and Hunting

The broch's coastal location gave its occupants easy access to marine resources. They caught fish, mostly small cod-family fish such as saithe and a few pollack, but also eel, flat-fish, sea scorpions and salmon or trout. Marine species could be caught from boats or from the shore, while freshwater fish were taken from inland lochs and rivers, perhaps with the aid of fish traps or weirs.

Fish may have been hung above the hearth in the centre of the broch to smoke. This method added flavour and preserved the fish so that it would last longer, providing a tasty source of protein through the lean winter and early spring.

Seal and whale were on the menu too. In spring, female seals come to shore to give birth to pups; they don't move fast on land, so they are easy to catch. Whales may have been hunted from small boats, but were also easily exploited when stranded on the shore. Carcasses washed up by the tide were worth using too. Meat, blubber bone, sinew: all of these were useful to an Iron Age family.

Photo by JOHNY REBEL, the Explorer Panda from Pexels

Seals were easy quarry in the spring, when females come to shore to give birth to their pups

Small cod-family fish like saithe may have been smoked over the fire

iStock.com/FedBul

Puffin and guillemot bones were found amongst the midden material in Cell 1, suggesting that these birds were eaten too. Both of these seabirds breed in large colonies, coming to shore only during the nesting season in the spring. At this time of year, they would have been relatively easy to catch with a net. They may have been desirable for their meat, eggs, feathers or fat.

Fishing, foraging and hunting added variety to the diet at Clachtoll

Limpets and periwinkles were gathered from the rocky shoreline, adding flavour and variety, and further calories when needed.

Puffin bones were found among midden material, suggesting that these birds were eaten

VisitScotland / Paul Tomkins

Berries like sloes added variety and flavour to the Iron Age diet

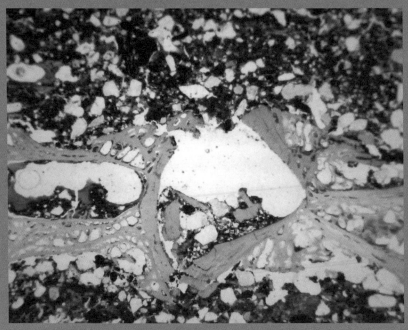

Microscopic evidence of a rodent problem: small mammal vertebrae embedded within floor deposits

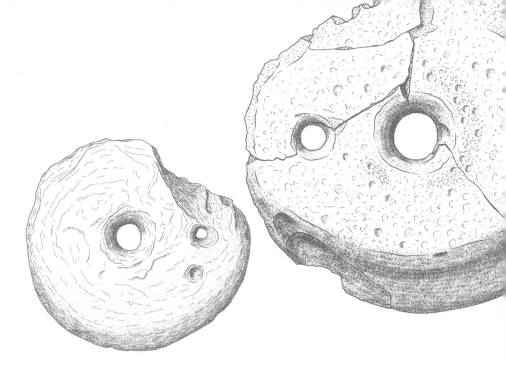

Hunting wasn't key to the economy at Clachtoll. Venison seems to have been an occasional treat, and though antler was an important resource, collecting shed antler would have been an easier and less risky way of gathering the raw material if the meat wasn't required.

Foraging for fruit and nuts would have added yet more variety: hazelnuts, crowberries and sloes. Species that we consider to be weeds – fat hen, chickweed and hemp nettle – may also have been gathered and cooked as vegetables, perhaps improving the flavour of cereal pottage. Evidence of beeswax suggests that honey from wild bees may have added sweetness to the diet at Clachtoll.

Pest Control

The animal bone evidence also gives a glimpse of uninvited guests in the broch. Rodent bones and coprolites – poo – within the floor deposits show that mice ran amok in the broch, though their numbers may have been kept in check by a pet cat or dog, evidenced only by gnaw-marks on discarded cow/sheep bones.

This reconstruction illustration shows how the interior of the broch might have looked when in use.

The central hearth provided light and heat, and fish may have been hung to smoke above it. The space around the hearth was divided into zones for everyday activities such as weaving and processing grain. We know where some of these activities took place due to the distribution of artefacts: spindle whorls, for example, were discovered in two distinct clusters.

The scarcement ledge would have supported a platform or upper storey of some kind. Any upper storeys, however, would not have extended across the full footprint of the broch. We might imagine them to be more like mezzanines, perhaps used as sleeping spaces or for storage.

The clerestory, to let light in and smoke out at the highest point of the roof, is entirely conjectural. We know very little about how brochs were roofed. However, the lack of windows means that brochs must have been quite dark inside, so an arrangement like this might have provided a little more light.

The illustration was produced by Chris Mitchell following discussions with AOC's archaeologists, and combines archaeological evidence with artistic license to give a glimpse of domestic life at Clachtoll.

Antler was a valuable raw material, probably gathered as shed antler rather than through hunting

Making and Doing:
Crafts at Clachtoll

An Iron Age farmstead's community like that at Clachtoll would have been pretty self-sufficient, in terms of food, but also in making everyday items. Evidence from the excavations shows that they made their own pots, spun yarn from wool, wove textiles, and made objects from antler and bone.

Pottery and Wooden Vessels

Around 250 sherds of hand-made pottery were found at Clachtoll, representing no more than 15 to 20 pots. The clay was most likely dug fairly locally; sources are known near Clachtoll beach. The upper portion of each of the vessels was decorated with impressed, incised or applied designs. On many of the pots, a trace of the potter's touch is visible in faint fingertip impressions left behind while shaping the malleable clay. The vessels were used for cooking or storage of foodstuffs, and most had everted (turned out) rims, perfect for pouring.

Wooden vessels were also made and used at the broch, evidenced by a piece of an unfinished alder bowl, shaped with an axe on the outside and roughly carved out on the inside.

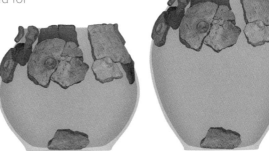

Excavation uncovered the remains of around 15-20 ceramic pots, which were made at the broch

Weaving and Spinning

Exceptional preservation of organic materials means that Clachtoll has yielded an exciting range of evidence for textiles and their production.

A short length of wool was recovered from a waterlogged deposit in one of the intramural cells. Close analysis shows that it was made from four strands of spun fleece, twisted together to form a cord. Organic materials like this usually disintegrate in the ground; it is very unusual to find wool preserved anywhere other than in peat bogs, making this small scrap of wool all the more special. It gives a rare, tangible link to the textiles that the people of Clachtoll were making, where usually we rely entirely on associated items – such as tools used to make textiles – to help us join the dots.

Evidence for spinning is present in the form of multiple stone spindle whorls, used to add weight to a slender wooden spindle to help it spin. What's more, the finds assemblage included over 30 objects identified as spindle whorls, with examples representing every stage of the production process, showing that they were made onsite.

Four long-handled combs, thought to have been used in textile production, show lots of wear

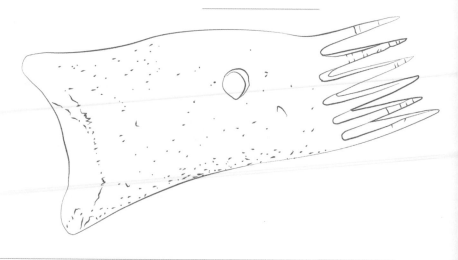

A short length of wool, preserved thanks to waterlogging

A short length of wool gives a rare, tangible link to textiles

Microscopic analysis revealed that the wool is formed of four twisted strands

More than 30 stone spindle whorls were discovered at Clachtoll

Bone combs survived in various conditions, from fragmentary to complete

Four complete or partial long-handled combs, thought to have been used in textile production, show lots of wear: one was so well-used that only one tooth remains. Close analysis of the teeth suggests that the combs served at least two different purposes: some may have teased out the tangles from fleeces, while others played a part in the weaving process. One of the combs shows significant wear around a perforation in its handle, suggesting that it was hung from a string or perhaps a leather thong. Perhaps this was so it could be hung up for storage, or it may even have been worn around the neck or at the waist, making sure it was always close at hand when needed.

Evidence of weaving yarn into textiles is less forthcoming. A perforated stone may have been used as a loom weight, tautening the vertical (warp) yarns on the loom. However, there are many other interpretations for a perforated stone like this, so it's hard to be certain about its function at Clachtoll.

There are also two bone needles used in sewing – both broken during use and discarded – and a handful of bone pins that would have held items of clothing together.

Antler & bone working

Fragments of bone and antler show that these materials were being worked at the site: a squared-off bar of cetacean bone had been roughly shaped so that it could be transformed into something else at a later date; and what might be an unfinished toggle made of a cattle phalanx (foot bone). Some of the bone and antler artefacts bear circular drilled perforations, suggesting that a bow-drill was used in their manufacture.

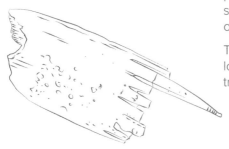

Whale bone anvil

Perhaps the most fascinating evidence of craft activities at Clachtoll comes in the form of an anvil or working surface made from a whale's vertebra. The upper surface is scarred by scores of toolmarks, incidental evidence of craft activities from two thousand years ago.

Close analysis of the toolmarks has led to the identification of at least four different tools including an axe or cleaver, a diamond-shaped punch and a circular punch. Peck marks, pits and shallow hollows suggest crushing or hammering activities.

Though the tools themselves no longer survive, their use can be traced in the marks left behind.

Whalebone Anvil Key	
● Red	hairline cracks caused by heat damage, probably while the broch burned down
● Blue	Deeper linear cuts, perhaps from the blade of an axe
● Purple	Punch with a diamond-shaped tip
● Green	Punch with a circular tip
● Orange	Linear chop marks, perhaps made with the sharp cutting edge of a metal cleaver
● Yellow ring	This ring-shaped area of wear is intriguing. It was caused by a crushing or pounding action. Could it be related to the shaping of spindle whorls?

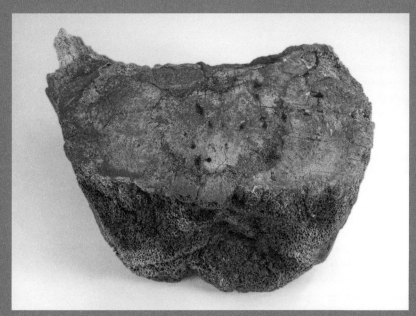

This whalebone vertebra was used as a working surface

*Close analysis of the surface reveals traces of
numerous tools and activities. Key to left.*

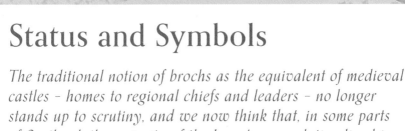

Status and Symbols

The traditional notion of brochs as the equivalent of medieval castles - homes to regional chiefs and leaders - no longer stands up to scrutiny, and we now think that, in some parts of Scotland, the majority of the Iron Age population lived in brochs and similar buildings. We know that Clachtoll was home to a farming community. However, one artefact found at the broch tells a story of status and connections: a bone pommel. The decoration on this pommel attests to long-distance connections in the aesthetics and symbolism of both everyday and prestige belongings.

This pommel was once fitted to the end of the hilt of a weapon, perhaps a dagger

A Prestige Pommel

A pommel is a rounded knob that was fitted to the end of the handle of a weapon such as a dagger or sword. The pommel from Clachtoll is quite small, suggesting that it may have once been part of a dagger rather than anything larger such as a sword. It is made of marine ivory (i.e. the tusk or tooth of a marine animal, probably a cetacean such as a whale) and ornamented on both sides with semi-ring-shaped grooves incised into the surface.

The finely-worked pommel is a prestige object, very different to the utilitarian, everyday bone artefacts made at the broch. Similar pommels have been found on a handful of sites across Atlantic Scotland and Ireland. The example from Clachtoll is almost certainly the result of trade or exchange, perhaps a gift from visitors, or an expensive souvenir from a trip further afield. Though we know the people of the broch were self-sufficient in lots of ways, the pommel gives a glimpse of wider networks of communication and the social status enjoyed by the people of Clachtoll, and is a rare example of an artefact from the broch that was desired more keenly for its aesthetics than for its practicality.

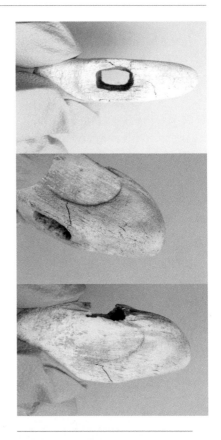

The pommel gives a glimpse of wider networks of communication and the social status enjoyed by the people of Clachtoll

Symbolism in Ceramics

The semi-circular design on the pommel is echoed in decoration on pottery found – and made – at Clachtoll. This type of circular decoration, found particularly on pottery from sites in the Hebrides, is known to have been created by pressing the ring-shaped head of a metal pin into wet clay. Perhaps one of Clachtoll's most exciting discoveries was an intact projecting ring-headed pin which matches exactly with the decorated pottery. With both pottery and pin, we can imagine the Iron Age potter pressing the head of the pin into the cold wet clay, working methodically around the pot's circumference to create an attractive design. The ring impressions are separated by zig-zagging lines cut into the clay with something sharp – the tip of the same pin, perhaps? The circular impressions may be interpreted as symbols of the sun, and are part of a wider tradition of decorative motifs with possible symbolic meaning that we can only guess at today.

Another sherd of pottery features a design that resembles cereal grains, perhaps made by pushing an ear of barley into the clay, or by using an implement to replicate the effect. Linear decoration above this pattern may represent the crops themselves, pushing up out of the ground. Taken together, this decorative design might reflect the community's reliance on agriculture, or perhaps on the nature of reproduction and fertility in general.

Wavy cordon decoration might represent the sea, a symbol of the undulating waves that were ever-present in the sea-scape, and sound-scape, of Clachtoll.

These decorative designs might relate to agriculture, perhaps depicting crops pushing their way upwards out of the earth

Sea

Land

Sky

Metal

Decorative symbols on pottery might have deeper meanings

A sherd of pottery, and the projecting ring-headed pin used to decorate it

The pin, moments after its discovery

The Broch in the Wider World

Prior to - and during - the final phase of occupation, Clachtoll was subject to remodelling, much like many other brochs. Its earliest rebuilds sought to reconstruct a broch tower, but its final incarnation was a much lower building, perhaps only around one and a half storeys high. This reduction in height might have been deliberate, but it is perhaps more probable that it was related to structural issues that the broch's final remodellers were unable to address. We might imagine that the community had seen broch towers elsewhere and wanted to associate themselves with a similarly monumental building, but were unaware of the complexity and subtlety of broch construction.

John Town

Some elements of the practices of which we find evidence within the broch are hard to interpret from our 21st century viewpoint. The remains of two sheep were buried inside the broch, close to the hearth, in what appears to have been a deliberate act of deposition. The sheep had been skinned and butchered but the carcasses were still articulated, with soft tissue remaining on the bones. Anyone who has ever had to live with the smell of a decomposing mouse beneath the floorboards will be able to imagine the olfactory effect of rotting sheep's carcasses within the home. However, this doesn't seem to have been a one-off. Similar deposits have been noted beneath floors and behind walls at other Middle Iron Age broch sites such as at the 'wheelhouses' at Sollas and Cnip, both in the Outer Hebrides and occupied at precisely the same time as Clachtoll. The intentional burial of a sheep within the home might relate to the community's close connection with agriculture and the flock – an offering to help bring about a good yield that year, perhaps – or might be linked to the symbolic completion of the house. In these directly comparable acts of deposition, over 100km apart, we see cultural and spiritual links between island and mainland communities, with shared rituals and practices.

The remains of two sheep were buried inside the broch in a deliberate act of deposition

Two sheep carcasses were buried inside the broch, seemingly in a deliberate act of deposition

Similarities in ceramic styles also indicate close contact between disparate communities. In the Iron Age, pottery was generally manufactured and used locally, rather than being made in bulk and sold widely. Nonetheless, people living across the north and west of Scotland chose to decorate their pots in the same way, using patterns and motifs that recur throughout this broch landscape.

These shared cultural links could reflect the movement of people, perhaps through marriage alliances or cross-community obligations. Such bonds between groups may have facilitated the sharing of resources required to build, maintain and supply key focal point settlements like Clachtoll.

Clashnessie Dun, 4.5km to the north-east of Clachtoll,
was in use at around the same time as the broch

A coastal stack seems an unlikely location for a building, but the Split Rock (the highest point shown here) was topped by some sort of structure in the Iron Age

Excavations in the Hinterland

As part of the project to explore Clachtoll, the project team undertook excavations at three nearby sites: the stack fort on the Split Rock; a dun (drystone enclosure) at Clashnessie; and the island settlement at Loch na Claise. Radiocarbon dating of samples from all of these sites returned dates contemporary with the occupation of the broch, and the known settlement sequence from the Stoer area seems to come to an end in the early years of the first millennium AD, around the time of the broch's demise. It's hard to make strong statements about possible links between the sites, but it would not be unreasonable to wonder whether the sites shared social or economic ties. When settlement at the broch ceased, this may have spelled the end of activity in the wider landscape.

The broch, in its final expression, was central to a productive and self-sustaining farmstead. The three satellite sites are much smaller, presumably home to smaller groups and perhaps to people who wielded less social clout than those at the broch. The storage of grain at Clachtoll may indicate that the broch's occupants controlled surplus yield. This might represent only their own crops, or could signify that they drew on resources from smaller settlements in the wider landscape, perhaps an indication of status and control. These smaller groups may have been tied to the broch, obliged to share their yield in return for tenancy of their lands, protection, access to produce and commodities, or other social bonds. Thus, when the broch burned down and its occupants moved on, the wider community moved on too.

We can only speculate on the circumstances around the fire at Clachtoll. It seems certain that the final fire took the broch's occupants by surprise. But was it the result of an unfortunate accident, a lapse of concentration, or a deliberate act of arson? The abandonment of the broch may even reflect a change in social structures, perhaps a new, more hierarchical system that rejected the broch tradition, so preventing the broch at Clachtoll from being rebuilt.

When the broch burned down and its occupants moved on, the wider community moved on too

Excavations on the Split Rock, 2017. The village of Clachtoll takes its name from the site's Gaelic place-name: A' Chlach Thuill, *'the hole stone'.*

This island in
Loch na Claise
was occupied
in the Iron Age

John Town

The broch sits in a rough and rocky landscape

Preparing the Broch for the Future

One of the main motivations behind the work at Clachtoll sought to prolong its survival. Not only had a chunk of its circumference been lost, but the pressure of the rubble inside the broch was pushing the walls outwards. The situation was becoming more precarious, both for the broch and for the safety of its visitors. Though no building can last forever, Historic Assynt and the local community were dedicated to maintaining one of the region's most iconic ancient monuments. All interventions aimed to enhance the broch's stability with minimal visual impact. Nonetheless, you might notice signs of these repairs when you visit the broch.

A steel frame provides support for a broken lintel

One of the primary areas in need of attention was the entrance. Earlier work by Historic Scotland had seen the repair of one of the lintels over the entrance passage, but continued movement within the structure had rendered the repair ineffective. An alternative solution was sought.

One of the lintels spanning the exterior entrance passage was split in two. It was removed prior to excavation of the passage and set aside for the duration of the works. On completion, the lintel was repaired before being replaced in its original location. Similarly, unstable lintels that spanned the stair gallery were labelled, removed, set aside during excavation and reinstated after the completion of consolidation work. A lot of the consolidation work was carried out in this way to retain as much of the broch's authentic character as possible.

The pressure of the rubble inside the broch was pushing the walls outwards

Before consolidation, the southern side of the broch was sliding down the sloping bedrock

The movement of the broch sliding down the sloping bedrock exerted enough pressure to snap the lintel of the doorway into one of the cells, and many of the stones above, creating a dangerous fissure in the stonework

The lintel at the entrance was precariously balanced

Rebuilding damaged stonework and installing steel supports has made the entrance safe

A master stonemason was onsite throughout the excavations, restoring areas of the broch where the stonework had become unstable. In some places, pressure and movement within the building had caused stones to crack and shatter, with jagged fissures running like lightning across the interior wall face. During the excavations, areas of concern were identified and rectified to make the building safe.

However, a more substantial intervention was needed at the southern side of the broch, where the stonework at the foot of the structure was essentially sliding down the slope of the rocky knoll. Here, a concrete plinth was inserted, supported by steel rods dowelled into the bedrock beneath, counteracting the slipping of the stonework and securing the wall above. A similar approach was taken to the broken wall ends, with the basal stones, behind the surviving debris slope, secured to the bedrock to prevent further movement that might bring about another collapse endangering the right hand guard cell.

Clachtoll Broch is now in a stable condition, and continues to endure being buffeted by Assynt's often harsh weather and crashing waves, as it has done for the last two thousand years. However, continued global warming is likely to increase the strength and power of winter storms which could continue to do further damage to the broch. Though no building can stand forever, work at Clachtoll has extended its life while giving us an opportunity to create a lasting record, and tell the broch's story.

The broch is now in a stable condition, and continues to endure being buffeted by Assynt's harsh weather and crashing waves

Large stones were moved with the aid of heavy lifting machinery

To tackle slippage at the southern side, temporary supports were installed in 2014 and replaced by a long-term solution, a concrete plinth, in 2017

Modelling the Past

The field of archaeology is taking great strides in using modern technological advances, to the benefit of our exploration - and preservation - of ancient monuments.

Global positioning systems – GPS – have been used in archaeology for many years in creating geolocated plans of archaeological sites. At Clachtoll, the location of every artefact was pin-pointed to allow for analysis of distribution, and identification of possible patterns which might represent activity areas.

Cutting-edge techniques contributed to every stage of the monitoring, preparation, excavation and analysis process

Mapping data was used in conjunction with 3D visualisation data to monitor the broch closely. 3D laser scanning has been used at every stage of the project. The creation of highly accurate digital models of the broch allowed for careful monitoring of the building's condition. Further models were made throughout the excavations, creating detailed records as rubble was removed from the interior.

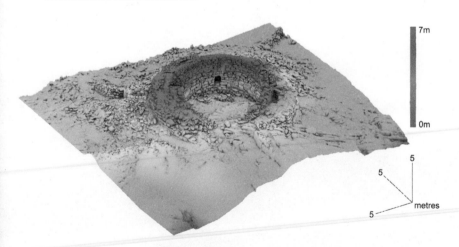

7m

0m

5

5

5

metres

The rainbow colours of this model are not just for effect; they indicate height

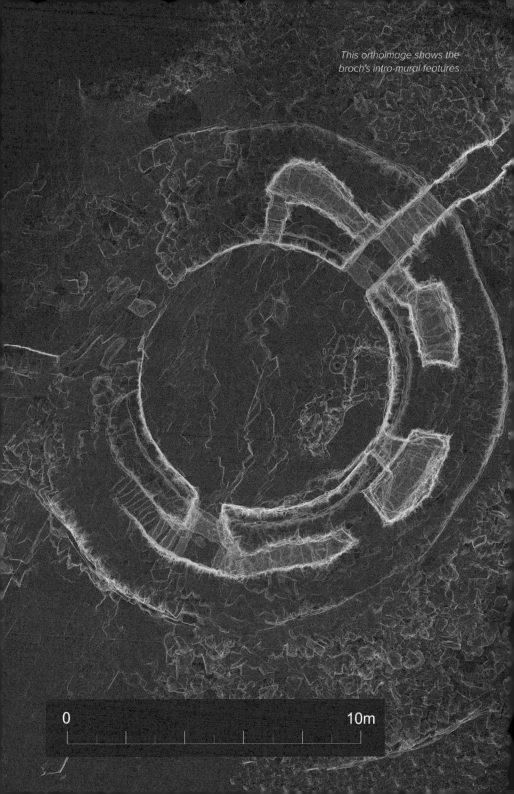

This orthoImage shows the broch's intra-mural features

0   10m

Whorls

● Spindle whorl

● Whorl, roughout or unfinished

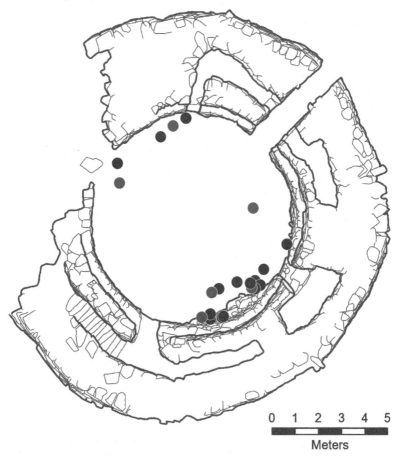

0 1 2 3 4 5

Meters

Spatial analysis helps us understand activity zones. Spindle whorls were found in two distinct clusters, suggesting that they were made and used in these areas (or directly upstairs, falling from above during the fire).

3D recording can used to document everything from wide-ranging landscapes to tiny artefacts. A selection of artefacts from the broch were recorded using photogrammetry, a technique that involves taking hundreds of photographs from every angle and meshing them together. The resulting 3D models can be made publicly available online, allowing anyone to examine an object or monument remotely.

The models can also be manipulated to create reconstructions. Multiple pottery sherds can be displayed together as they might have appeared as part of an intact vessel. Researchers can take digital replicas of fragmentary objects and piece them back together without any risk of damage to the originals.

This highly accurate data can also be used to create 3D printed replicas. A selection of artefacts from Clachtoll have been reproduced in this way, the 3D models painstakingly hand-painted to replicate the originals as closely as possible. These replicas can be used for teaching since they can be handled freely, and they can be displayed anywhere since they do not require climate-controlled conditions like their 2000-year-old counterparts.

Cutting-edge techniques contributed to every stage of the monitoring, preparation, excavation and analysis process. The digital data can be made accessible on online platforms, to enable others to conduct their own research on the broch and its objects from afar, bringing an ancient monument in the north-west of Scotland within reach of anyone who wants to explore it.

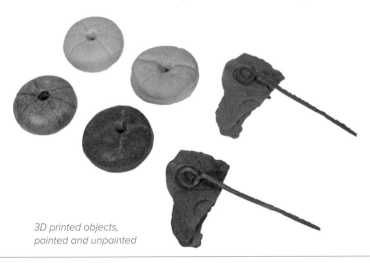

3D printed objects, painted and unpainted

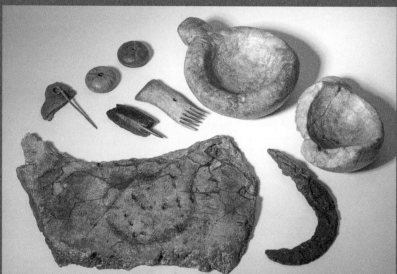

3D printing produces replica artefacts which can be handled and displayed without risk of damage to the often fragile originals

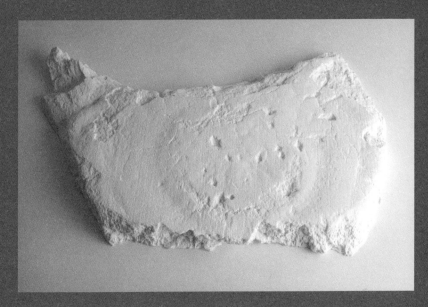

Before and after: the 3D prints are carefully hand-painted to represent the original artefacts' colours and textures

Exceptional archaeology and a
team of dedicated and tireless
volunteers made for a busy and
fulfilling community excavation

A Project for All of Assynt

The excavations at the broch provided the perfect starting point for an exciting programme of events so that the wider community could enjoy opportunities to engage with the archaeology of Assynt, from training workshops to celebratory Iron Age feasts.

Volunteers were involved in all aspects of the excavation, receiving training as they worked. Opportunities for participation in the post-excavation process saw volunteers cataloguing finds and sorting the flot (floating ecofacts such as charcoal and cereal grains) and retents (small stones and artefacts) from soil samples, sifting through and sorting the material to extract tiny clues to the broch's past.

An artist in residence guided children and adults through the process of bronze casting. They created designs in local beeswax, inspired by what the broch means to them. Their designs were cast in bronze using pre-industrial methods, and included copper smelted on the beach by Ullapool High School students and others. The resulting 44 bronze sculptures have been placed in the landscape close to the broch, for visitors to discover.

The project aimed to encourage people to take ownership of the area's heritage by helping them experience it in exciting and engaging ways

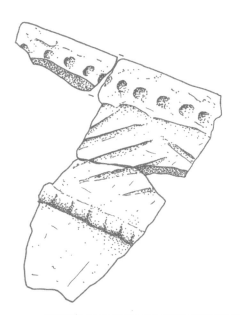

Roz Summers

Workshops saw the creation of Iron Age-style pottery, made and fired outdoors

Roz Summers

An artist in residence guided children and adults through the process of bronze casting

Gordon Sleight

Bronzes can be found in the landscape near the broch, made during workshops with the project's artist in residence

A stimulating schools programme was put together and delivered in a collaboration between CALLP's learning team, AOC's archaeologists and numerous others including Highland Council's ranger Andy Summers, and local ecologist Roz Summers. Pupils from the local primary schools visited the broch to see the excavations in progress, learning about the broch itself and the people who lived there. They had a chance to try their hand at digging, excavating test pits in the broch's hinterland. High school pupils participated in an Iron Age Survival School: foraging on the seashore provided an opportunity to explore what marine resources might have been available to the broch's community, exploring hot stone technologies, and trying traditional skills while testing how the roof of the broch may have been constructed. After the end of the excavations, high school pupils also learned about the post-excavation process in a hands-on workshop that explored what archaeologists can learn from artefacts, ecofacts and tree-ring dating.

Experimental archaeology helped answer some of the questions thrown up by the excavations. Under the watchful eye of AOC's John Barber, archaeologists and volunteers created a corbelled stone structure close to the broch, testing our understanding of this technique (and perhaps creating an attractive home for some of Clachtoll's otter population). Experimental use of wattle panels for creating upper storeys in the broch involved weaving substantial panels, testing their weight-bearing capabilities, and finally setting them alight to see how swiftly they burned (very, as it turns out!).

Though the excavations themselves leave a lasting physical legacy in the radically altered appearance – and hoped-for longevity – of the broch, these experiences will, we hope, stay with those who were involved in Clachtoll Broch Project for a long time. The project aimed to encourage people to take ownership of the area's heritage by helping them experience it in exciting and engaging ways, with the broch at the heart of this objective. The broch remains an enduring symbol of a community's achievements, in prehistory and today.

*The broch remains
an enduring symbol
of a community's
achievements,
in prehistory
and today*

*Visitors were welcomed to the broch
with tours of the archaeology while
excavations were underway*

Experiments in building (and burning) contributed to interpretation of the excavated deposits

Acknowledgements

Any acknowledgements must, of course, include an enormous thank you to all the volunteers who took part in the excavations (without whom we would still be removing rubble to this day), experimental archaeology, finds cataloguing and many other elements of the project. The project's success is due to the commitment and passion of everyone who gave their time and energy, and to you we extend our gratitude.

Local Superstars

Robin Noble, then chair of Assynt Community Council, who got Historic Assynt involved in the first place and did the bulk of the work for the initial feasibility study

Assynt Crofter's Trust, Crofter Iain Matheson and subsequently his daughter Katie, for leasing the broch site to Historic Assynt

The many local people who participated in the various public meetings and consultations and whose opinions and concerns have contributed to the development of the project and also those who contributed their skills and time to the wide range of archaeological experiments and public events during the course of the project, especially Marc Campbell and Fergus Stewart.

The staff and membership of CALLP, the Coigach and Assynt Living Landscape Partnership, and lead partner the Scottish Wildlife Trust. The 2017-2021 Broch Project is just one of many projects within that partnership, and the support and involvement of CALLP has been crucial for the project's success.

Broch Liaison Officers for both 'Life and Death in Assynt's Past' and the current project: Brenda Gibson, Sharon Bartram, Mandy Haggith, Richard Pease, Roz Summers

A Note from AOC

This list of acknowledgements and thanks was put together by Gordon Sleight, previously chair of Historic Assynt, and far too modest to acknowledge his own role in work at Clachtoll. Gordon was instrumental to the success of Clachtoll Broch Project, driving the project forward from conception to completion with commitment, perseverance and a great deal of patience. He has now relinquished his role to Dave McBain, who continues to steer Historic Assynt towards exciting ventures. We would like to extend our heartfelt thanks to Gordon, Dave and all at Historic Assynt – and indeed the wider Assynt community – for involving us in work at Clachtoll.

Funders

National Lottery Heritage Fund (LDAP and current projects)

Historic Environment Scotland (LDAP and current projects)

SSE Sustainable Development Fund

Pilgrim Trust

Highland Council, for a grant towards this publication, as well as wider support of the project through the Scottish Landfill Communities Fund

Lund Trust

Robert Kiln Trust

Highland Leader (LDAP only)

Private donors

Leadership, Consultancy and Supervision

AOC Archaeology Group, particularly John Barber, Graeme Cavers, Andy Heald and Pat Buchanan for their involvement throughout

Brian Wilson, Dimitris Theodossopoulos and all those who have done specialist work like engineering consultancy, coring etc.

Architects and fabricators involved in the access provision:
Cristina Gonzalez-Longo, Cameron Webster Architects,
PLD Smiddy Ltd

HES Officers involved in the regular meetings/consultations

Coigach & Assynt Living Landscape Partnership

Scottish Wildlife Trust